THE WORDS WE SHARE

THE WORDS WE SHARE

A Book of Poems

TOBIAS GALE

Copyright © 2024 by Tobias Gale

All rights reserved. No part of this book may be reproduced or used in any manner without written permission of the copyright owner except for the use of quotations in a book review.

Front cover image by Tobias Gale
Cover design by Christine Horner
Book design by Iram Allam
Edited by Brittany Ringler

ISBN 978-1-7349774-4-8

Library of Congress Control Number: 2023920655

Published in Boulder, Colorado

www.tobiasgale.com

CONTENTS

PREFACE	ix
AT THE BEGINNING	1
TREASURE	2
GALAXY	3
THE WHISPER	4
THE CALL	5
THE DOOR	6
MYSTERY	7
GAME OF WAITING	8
HOW LONG?	9
INTO THIS MOMENT	10
THAT ANOTHER SUFFERS	11
PRAYER OF THE HEART	12
I WAIT	14
WITHIN	15
NOTHING LEFT	16
A FISH	17
THE WORLD I SEE	18
A CALL FOR LOVE	19
BROTHER	20
LONGING FOR RELEASE	22
TO LOVE YOU	23

TO BE FILLED	24
THE HEART THAT CONNECTS	25
MY GIFT TO YOU	26
TWO BECOMES ONE	27
TOGETHER	28
SUNLIGHT	29
ONLY YOUR CHILD	30
NOTHING MORE, NOTHING LESS	31
EVERY MOMENT	32
PEACE WAITS	33
BECOMING	34
DESERT	35
ONCE MORE	36
UNAWARE	37
CAN I STAY?	38
MY SHADOW	40
LAYER BENEATH LAYER	41
THE PROMISED LAND	42
I AM HERE	43
THE OCEAN	44
TO WANDER	45
BE CLOSE	46
THE GREAT CRY	47
THE FACE OF MY MOTHER	48
THE GREAT DIVIDE	49
BEYOND THE WORLD	50
BORN AGAIN	51
BEAUTY OF MY HEART	52
THE MOON	53
TO LIFE	54

A PLACE TO LAND	55
A WRITER	56
EVERY STEP	57
MY LITTLE, LONELY WORLD	58
DEEP IN YOU	59
WITHOUT YOU	60
THE MEANING AND THE GIFT	61
GUIDED BY LOVE	62
NEW LIFE	63
WATER IN THE WILDERNESS	64
TRUE NATURE	65
MEANDERINGS OF MY SOUL	66
ETERNAL LOVE	67
TRUE WIND	68
A BIRD	69
FOOTSTEPS	70
HERE TO STAY	71
HOLINESS	72
IN SILENCE	73
STARS	74
THE GARDEN	75
IN GLORY	76
HEART OF LOVE	77
INFINITE	78
ALREADY THERE	79
AWAKE	80
NO END IN YOU	81
AS I AM	82
AT THE END	83

PREFACE

Poetry is particularly effective at facilitating a spiritual experience, as in the psalms of David, the parables of Jesus, or the devotional writings of Rabindranath Tagore. It illuminates a doorway that invites the reader into the mysticism the author experienced and sought to articulate, where the words are not chosen by the mind, but the soul. Transmissions of this kind are effective because they are received by the soul of the reader, bypassing the intellect. To offer an experience of this kind is one of the profound gifts of poetry.

I started writing poetry many years ago, when I simply wrote the words my soul wanted to speak. I let him be my guide, and let God—the Spirit within—be my guide, and I was gathered and held in that transcendent place, the eternal warmth of divine expression, creation, unification. I knew then that I was a poet and that my poetry (or rather, the poetry that came through me) was actively transforming me, and could transform those who read it.

The Words We Share is a collection of poems I began writing in 2015 and finished in 2022. It encapsulates my own spiritual journey of suffering, longing, devotion, and transcendence. And it describes what I believe to be many seekers' journey, hence the title of my book. This journey, while not linear, moves in a forward direction, and I sought to arrange my poems in this way.

I encourage you to let the reading of these poems be an *experience*. Like a meditation, give yourself the time and space to just *be* with them. Each poem is *for you*. Let the words you read and their meaning move within you. Notice what arises. Whatever feelings are there, cherish them. They are the doorway to your *Life*.

THE WORDS WE SHARE

AT THE BEGINNING

At the beginning of time
God whispered to me,

"I Love You."

TREASURE

I covered something in me long ago.
I was scared and so I hid it;
I didn't want its preciousness revealed
and then taken away.

But many years have passed
and I've forgotten it.

At times I'm reminded of the treasure in me,
when I see beauty in the world
and recognize its source.
Then I remember.

Where is it now? I ask.
Somewhere deep within me?
Can what was hidden still be revealed?
And if revealed, kept?

GALAXY

In the galaxy, when I was young,
I saw all the stars and planets
and could hardly speak—

How could something so beautiful
come from so much pain?

THE WHISPER

Before I knew of Light
I could not differentiate one from the other.
My life was not known to me;
the "I" of me had not begun.

Only vibration.
Only openness.

I heard in the whisper a Voice,
more like a passing breeze than a clear and audible tone.
There was no language in it,
no sense to be made by it.

Only a feeling—
an awakening.

Is there something beyond or within this? I thought.
Is it my own voice I hear?
(Though I do not know what it means to make sound,
or to create something from nothing.)

Am I that which was whispered to,
or am I the whisper?

THE CALL

I didn't tell anyone where I was going,
or why.

The path that I follow
is the path that leads me into the desert.
It is not a desert of wandering,
for I have wandered,
and the wandering has brought me here.

It is a desert that asks me to look
and to feel all the many aspects of my being,
all that has built me unto this day,
and all that has left me in my many lives.
This, I know, is the reason I've been called to go.

And yet, I'm scared.
I'm scared to heed this call.
I'm scared of what I'll find in the depths of my being.
I'm scared of the darkness when I walk away
from Your light.
I'm scared of myself when I believe in the emptiness
stretched out before me.

THE DOOR

The greatest loss is to forget the open space
where God rests within us;
to have awareness of a door,
but to believe it will never open.

MYSTERY

"Who will complete me, if not myself?"
thought the boy lost in the forest.

Can the Great Hand touch what doesn't know itself
to be already whole?
Does the mystery dissolve in the knowing
or in the letting go?

GAME OF WAITING

It doesn't always come;
I don't always see You.

I may sit for a while,
lost in the stories of my mind.
Time will elapse,
and for a moment I'll remember my intention—
that I am here to remember You,
to love You,
to return to You.

There is a child in me, tugging at my shirt,
telling me it's time to go,
that no one is coming for us—
to stop this game of waiting.

As long as it is a game of waiting
no one will ever come.

HOW LONG?

How long must I wait
till I see the light of Your face
and feel the fullness of Your love?

My heart yearns for You.
My longing overflows in sadness and tears.
My life feels barren and my dreams are lost.
I wander in darkness, naked and without shelter.

In brief moments You remind me of our love,
of resting together by the fire,
like the warmest dog,
the smell of burning sage,
or the nourishment that comes from a slow drink of tea.

My God, I love You.
From the darkened place
where I lie naked and without comfort,
I love You.

INTO THIS MOMENT

You call me back into this moment,
to the place where I can finally let go.

I see You here, in the endless light and colors
that You bring.
I hear You here, with all the sounds of love and pain,
and the world that is the echo of our imagination.
I feel You here, like a cavern swept through with water,
a desert baking in sunlight,
or a forest quiet to the life within.

Keep me here, my Love.
Keep me here.
Let not my wounds take me from this fertile ground.
Help me choose this place as home.
Help me choose again.

THAT ANOTHER SUFFERS

That another suffers as I suffer,
that another seeks You as I seek You—
this is the glory,

Amen.

PRAYER OF THE HEART

When he walked into the temple
I only heard him.
My eyes were closed as I listened to my heart.
I imagined what he thought, and how he judged me,
seeing my hands in prayer.

Is there no peace, acceptance, or understanding
for a man's yearning for God?
Is it not known yet that the fire in our souls is
burning out,
that the prayer of the heart must be seen and spoken?

I returned to stillness,
knowing he was there,
maybe watching
or listening to my unheard cries.

And I thought,
perhaps he too seeks You, God, as I seek You.
Perhaps he too suffers, as I suffer.
Perhaps this temple is not mine alone,
but for us all to enter and rest,
to wander, and then be still.

I opened my eyes.
And as I was walking out I saw him there,
sitting as I was sitting,
his hands resting to receive;
his face turned upward and inward
for the same peace and blessing that I sought.

I WAIT

When I close my eyes,
so gently You appear,
like the softest light.

It seems my days are a striving
to rest in that space where we are alone
and You tell me how much You love me.

I close my eyes and seek refuge in You.

I wait, I wait,
I wait.

WITHIN

No wind comes through these walls.
I have forgotten how to knock,
and how to open.

There is a garden within,
and I cannot enter.
In my own house, I cannot enter.

NOTHING LEFT

There is nothing left.
The seeds have emptied
themselves onto some ground,
and I do not know where they are
or what will become of them.

A FISH

You are not a fish drawn from water.
If you are a fish, you are deep down in the ocean current,
basking in the glimmer of light.

And yet I see you tossing about,
not knowing where the water is
that you were drawn from.
I try to pick you up to bring you back,
but you wiggle from my hands
and fall to the hard ground.

I fear that time will cast its permanency on you,
and that the waters will become a memory and recede.
I fear you will forget you are a fish,
and grow arms and legs and walk on land.
I fear you will forget how to breathe in water,
and that you'll wander endlessly
for all the days of your life.

This is my fear.
This is my sadness.

THE WORLD I SEE

Sometimes as a Child
I remember who I am—
that God is my God,
and the stars are lights
upon my bedroom ceiling.

But other times the world is dark
and I lose sight of its meaning.
I wrap myself in garments
and pretend that I'm alone.

Mother, have you found me yet,
hiding in the trees?
For I am no longer in love
with the world I see.

A CALL FOR LOVE

In this darkness I become something I am not,
turned from the light
and scattered into loneliness.

Whoever taught me to walk away from Your grace?
Why do I build walls around my nakedness,
leaving no room for Your memory?

How I wish to be rid of this false self
and bring love to the scared child inside me;
how I wish to forgive the monster, misguided and afraid,
and look beneath its mask
to see the pain and beauty there.

How I wish to know there is no monster,
that the harm I cause myself and others is a call for love,
a call for peace,
a call for You to take me back into Your loving arms
so I may rest.

BROTHER

On the morning of your birth,
at the very moment you sprang forth into this world,
there came with you a brother.
You did not know him,
for he was with you as God is with you,
but his presence was a shadow in the light of your soul.

As your mother and father looked into your eyes,
he was there,
praying he was good enough to be loved.
As the truth in you sung out,
his voice was hushed by generations past,
by the hurt carried from life to life,
pressed into the caverns of his yearning.

In the beginning, he was like you.
But over time the world no longer saw his wings,
so they receded.
And the world no longer heard his song,
so it was quieted.
And the world no longer saw his light,
so he walked in darkness.

Is this the enemy you speak of?
For there is no enemy here,
not in you, nor in him.
If there is an enemy,
it is the fear that told him he wasn't good enough,
that said his wings were not wings
and his song was no song.
If there is an enemy,
it is the fear that comes from angels gathered together,
who have forgotten that they too have wings
and that their light still flickers
in the long hallway of time.

LONGING FOR RELEASE

I have lost at winning every time;
at conquering;
at surpassing the ways that require deep, slow turning;
at overriding impulses learned
in the desperate race away from death.

I have lost at flying beyond where I am called to fly,
and at falling in ways that are graceful and forgiving.
I have lost at claiming my wings and my light,
and at opening to Your love like an endless cup.

And yet, I am here, still.
Not gone, nor lost,
but one speaking to the soul of souls,
crying into the great wind,
and longing for release.

TO LOVE YOU

Let me not be afraid to love You, God,
for my heart is open
and I fear I'll be seen and laughed at.

Let me not be afraid to love You, God,
for I see the world's pain
and I fear they'll point fingers and blame me.

Let me not be afraid to love You, God,
for I yearn to raise my arms in freedom
and dance in the wild grass.

Let me not be afraid to love You, God,
for I cannot help but love You.

TO BE FILLED

Resting in You,
every nerve is calmed;
my heart beats at a pace
that knows the rhythm of Your voice.
I sink down into You,
and am lulled into a wakeful dream.

When can we meet again?
When can I live in You?
When will I awaken to the remembrance
that we have never left one another—
that we swim together,
laugh together,
and open our hearts to be filled?

THE HEART THAT CONNECTS

I heard Her speak to me at night,
in the echoes of my room.

A rock I had placed between my Child and me,
not purposefully,
but while in search of what I feared was lost.

My words and actions became mute,
removed of all their color and warmth.
I looked out into the world from eyes no longer mine.

"Heal the wounds of your Child," She said,
"but not alone—this you cannot do alone.
For it is in your aloneness that you forget
the Heart that connects you to all things."

MY GIFT TO YOU

Wait, my child.
Desire calls to you
as if the world could run out of love.
But the blessings of this moment will fade
if not cherished now.

The bird that sings will not sing the same song.
The light that shines will not shine again like this.

The tears that you cry,
let them fall
and be a doorway into your soul.

Let not the world stop you from receiving what is yours.
Let not desire keep you from all that's here right now.

Wait my child,
wait.

The Door is open—
it is my gift to you.

TWO BECOMES ONE

You need not look for Me anywhere
but in your own experience,
just as it is.

In this moment,
in all things,
I am that which touches that;

the meeting of two becomes One,
and all that is anything becomes a part of Me.

TOGETHER

Together—
I can't do this, except together.
My world cannot run, except when together.

If I wander,
please bring me back.
When I lose sight of this moment,
please bring me back.

For so long I looked at the clouds,
the thunder, the rain,
and blamed it on something or someone, this or that.
But I am the maker of these weather patterns.
Separate from myself, the storms roll in—
together, there is peace.

SUNLIGHT

Dance on me, Sunlight.
Show me the ways of freedom and love.

Seep into me.
Let my body become a haven for Your presence.

Stay with me.
Let my mind be an open stretch of earth for You to bless,
so that my thoughts may sing,
and my actions may uplift the soul within me.

ONLY YOUR CHILD

Take me back to the place of my birth,
before birth,
before knowing.

In the arms of unconditional love,
I am only Your Child.

NOTHING MORE, NOTHING LESS

We can come back to that place
where all those things no longer matter.
The becoming of this, the losing of that—
we can let go of all that now.

The foundation has been built
and all the earth and heavens support us.

That story that could never be finished—
let it be complete in never being finished.
For like everything else, it's just a story.

The Heart of Grace is open to us,
but in it, we can only bring ourselves.
Nothing more, nothing less.

EVERY MOMENT

I only have this one moment to see Your face,
to look at the flower
and know that the flower is in me.
I only have this one moment
to be with the clouds in their color and expansion,
lest the skies darken and the clouds fade into night.

I've lived as though each day holds the same glory,
as though the beauty of every sight and sound,
of every feeling and connection,
was just another of hundreds that would come again.
But You are so miraculous that every moment is unique.
No cloud is ever like another;
no flower, no face, no love, no loss,
ever comes again in the way it does.
And each has its own special love.

PEACE WAITS

Tell me,
when you've done everything you've set out to do,
checked off every item from the list,
will that be enough?
Will peace finally come then?

As you move from one thing to the next,
looking for that space in time
when the world no longer needs your attention,
peace waits.

BECOMING

Let me stop searching, oh God.
Let me stop becoming.
Help me learn there is no need to search,
no need to become.

Day by day the voice pushes upon me,
telling me there's more to do.

Help me know the truth, oh God,
and bring this truth into my soul,
so that my living may be its own becoming,
so that my doing may be the work of this holy unfolding.

DESERT

I asked Him how long it would take
to get through the desert.

He couldn't tell me.

Again, and again I would ask, *"How long?
How long?"*

It was a miserable experience.
There was nothing there—

just a barren desert.

ONCE MORE

At times, I feel a wall between us without end.
I look and look for that opening,
the doorway into You,
but it is gone.

To know You in Your closeness,
and then to forget Your warmth,
is to be left without the spark that draws me back.

Even as I write, it is with an emptiness.
The wall has closed me off from You.
And now I hardly remember the love You gave me,
how it lifted me into the heavens,
how your gentle touch held my tears,
softened the edges of my anger,
and helped me to surrender once more.

UNAWARE

It's when I acknowledge You that I am here,
and everything in me comes to the surface.
Oh, there's the sadness that was caught beneath my fears;
there's my tired soul.

How difficult it is to come to You—
to just come,
leaving the weight of me at the door
and following You into the opening.

Always here, You are,
entering me and loving me,
and so often I am unaware.

CAN I STAY?

Can I stay?
In the movements of my heart
and in the bitterness of my Child's fear?
Can I stay?
In the sweat and pulling of the day
and in the quiet coolness of the night?

Can I be alone with You?
Through all the trials of my life?
Through every break and union?
As the sea threatens to overtake the earth?
As the desert seems to last an eternity?

In this drought
can I be fed by only Your sweet rain?
Can I place my naked trust
in Your forever hands?

Can I give up the weight that my freedom lies
in some place not already here?
That a cure can be found
at some time not already now?

Can I let go of this prison
that my shadow is my enemy?
That my Child was given to me without my consent?
(As if Your will was thrust upon me
to be a chain and a curse,
rather than a flower and a blessing.)

Who am I to judge Your eternal plan?
Who can know the path that treads before them?

Come back into these waters You tell me,
and with resistance I return.
When will I remember that Your will to return
is my blessing?
That there is no loss in coming back home?

MY SHADOW

Come my Child,
my shadow, my love.
No longer walk behind me, or apart from me.
I did not cast you to the ground.
I did not say, "Be ashamed,"
or "Never can you meet me in the midday sun."

A lie was spoken,
the clouds gathered,
and the darkness drew itself up
and took you from me.

Let go of him.
Let him be mine.
I am He who was called the Father,
who bore him from my breast,
opening me to changing seasons,
to love and loss.

Come my Child, come—
no more my shadow,
than my deepest love.

LAYER BENEATH LAYER

Layer beneath layer,
soul within soul,
this is how God becomes known.
This is how *we* are known.

What becomes of me when I move down
beneath the layers of myself?
How much sound will come from me?

A shofar of sound—
the unraveling of a great storm.

THE PROMISED LAND

There are no gates that lead into Your Kingdom,
yet every hour that I pass Your door
is a gate I place between us.

I look into houses that are not my own for treasures.
I read books for glimpses of the Promised Land.
I envy those who've found teachers,
received visions,
or appear without obstacles to Your love.

And all the while, I neglect to see the treasure
You've placed in my own heart,
and how it is Your presence
that has warmed the walls of this temple.

I AM HERE

I am here,
as you wait in the fields, upon the hill,
with the wind gently touching your skin,
with the air, still and bright—
I am here.

I am here,
when darkness seems to fall and surround you.
I am here,
when anxiety clings to you and does not let go.
I am here,
when sadness wells up within your heart and stays.

I am here,
during all these times
when you feel alone and abandoned,
lost and afraid.
I am here,
and have never left you.

THE OCEAN

The Ocean calls to me, patient and loving.
Yet I am stubborn, seeking my own way to Its shore.
I stumble and fall, and am covered in remnants
of my doing,
blinded by desire,
tempted by distraction.

But I will fall into You, God—
I stumble, so I might fall into You.

TO WANDER

It is a curious thing, isn't it?
To wander....
To know Home,
and not be there.

BE CLOSE

Born into this world You brought me,
carrying me in Your loving arms.
Oh Father, Mother, God of me, be close.
Be close in this world of shadow and form.

THE GREAT CRY

My tears are not my own.
My grief is not my own.

We all share in the great cry
that echoes through the ages,

through time and beyond time,
endlessly searching for Hashem.

THE FACE OF MY MOTHER

I see the pain in my mother's face—
a hidden pain,
a forgotten pain.
Millions of moments pushed away;
cries that echo into an endless night.

Who would hear my cry if I cried?
Who would love my soul in her nakedness?

The river stretches far beyond what we can see,
moving in currents and over rocks,
flowing with fish and rotten leaves,
carrying it all.
Nothing is forgotten or left behind.

I look into the face of my mother, and she cries.

THE GREAT DIVIDE

From sleep, I tried to cross the great divide.
Only it was endless,
and I eventually gave up.

On my way back,
feeling hopeless and in despair,
I stopped, and I cried.

Tears ran down my face,
warm and free.
I breathed in a generous breath,
and the earth no longer felt so bleak.

My aloneness gave way to closeness,
and in that moment I knew I had made it.

BEYOND THE WORLD

I seek to go beyond the world,
to dive deep into God and not return.
Not to be lost, but to be found in God;
to open, to awaken,
to smile at life from the depths of this peace.

In the opening all things are transformed.
Darkness into light,
sadness into joy,
anguish into faith.

I become the place where love manifests;
I become the voice that speaks holy truths;
I become the mother who carries God's eternal child.

BORN AGAIN

Born again;
after the fall, I am born again.

Too long have I wandered between two worlds.

Now is the time, and I must jump,
to fall,
so I may be reborn.

BEAUTY OF MY HEART

By what storm,
by what blessing have I been laid bare?

For only in my nakedness
can I see myself
and know the beauty of my heart.

THE MOON

I am naked,
and the Moon does glow for me.
I am a song,
and the Moon does glow for me.
I am etchings carved in the wood,
and the Moon does glow for me.

I am anger and a lost melody,
and the Moon does glow for me.
I am tired roots praying to be released from the soil,
and the Moon does glow for me.
I am a heart squeezed out and left deserted,
and the Moon does glow for me.

I am God and God's child,
and the Moon does glow for me.
I am the serpent, misunderstood,
and the Moon does glow for me.
I am Adam, who believed a fearful lie,
and Eve, the mother of all things,
forever in the womb of eternity,
and the Moon does glow for me.

TO LIFE

Just when I think the river has dried up
and no more flowers will grow from these shores,
You send down the clearest water,
and all the earth returns to life.

A PLACE TO LAND

Make me a house with no inner walls,
so that the river may run through me uninhibited.
So that when there is a cry, there is a place to land.
So that where there is friction, there is space.

A WRITER

I do not write to be a writer.
I write because the soul asks me to write,
and so I write.

I do not write for the praise of others.
I write because God has called me to the front door,
whispering words to me that cannot be contained.

I do not write for love,
but from the heart that swells in the touching
of this moment
and releases its cares to a world unseen.

Alas, have I become a writer in the answering of this call?
But it is not so much me who writes, but *We* who writes.

EVERY STEP

Walk into the wilderness gently.
Let God know you're there.
And let every step speak
and tell the story of who you are.

MY LITTLE, LONELY WORLD

You are my angel,
for You have given me safety.
In a world of tremendous beauty,
You have helped me see it.

The owl that flew past me the other night,
silent as the air—was that You?
Letting me know You are not just behind me,
but in front of me, and on all sides?

The river You took me to
that was the embodiment of peace—
You showed me that everything is God
when I drop down from my high seat
and let myself go.

Looking into Your eyes,
I am reminded there is only one moment.
Why chase a dream
when Heaven has opened inside and outside
what was my little, lonely world?

DEEP IN YOU

Deep,

deep,

deep in You I find my peace.
Deep in You I am reborn.

Light shines down
gently upon me.

I am no longer a hindrance to myself,
but an empty vessel to be filled.

WITHOUT YOU

Where would I be without You?
Who could I be without You?

The days that pass are like papers in the wind;
each morning, a new face,
lost in the crowd of time and fear.

Without You,
Love could not be what it is—
rich and tender,
vulnerable and open.

Without You,
Peace could not be what it is—
quiet and clear,
soft and light.

Without You,
the depths of my soul could not be felt—
not without You telling me, in the kindest voice,
"It's okay, I'm here."

Where would I be without You?
Who could I be without You?

THE MEANING AND THE GIFT

There is no peace, nor love, nor joy
apart from God.

God is the Love that extends from me to you;
God is the Joy that sings to me with eyes closed;
God is the Peace that comes over me in stillness;
God is the meaning and the gift.

GUIDED BY LOVE

Do what is most loving—
loving in the moment,
always in the moment.
And the long decision,
which stretches beyond what you can see,
will be made without confusion or strain.

Attend to this moment,
this feeling of tiredness,
of discontent,
of seeking another way out.
The day is only this.
Your life is only what's in front of you.
And he said, "Know what is in front of your face,"
"Seek first the Kingdom of God"—
not hidden, but in front of you;
within and without.

Where else is there to go, but here?
What else to attend to, but now?
Holy within, holy without.
The decision makes no difference,
as long as it is guided by love.

NEW LIFE

All that is ever asked,
if we desire the truth to enter us
and make us new again,

is to turn to what is.
And it is tender,
and there is love,
and we are born again into new life.

WATER IN THE WILDERNESS

There is water in the wilderness.
It runs like any brook or stream.
If you are loud, it will go unheard.
If you are hasty, it will go unnoticed.

But if you are still,
if you are quiet,
if your walk is gentle and your heart is open,
then you cannot help but come upon it.

There in the wilderness it is,
and all who come in thirst are quenched.
The forest becomes a place of light,
and everything in it becomes a friend.

TRUE NATURE

Listen—

to the wind, to the birds,
to the silent space between all things.

This is God.

In the deepest rest,
all things return to their true nature.

MEANDERINGS OF MY SOUL

Can I tell you of the season I've found within me?

Oh, the birds are glorious,
the flowers forever in bloom,
and the waters flow like sweet rain.

May the air you breathe remind you of this season.

In the meanderings of my soul,
I let my hand brush against the walls—
a cavern, endless as it runs deep into the center.
Can you see the light reflected there?
Against these tear-wetted walls?
So beautiful.

I don't mind if you come with me—
I've travelled so many years alone.
I know the sanctity of this temple.
I know it keeps me and loves me.

ETERNAL LOVE

I have not forgotten you, my Child,
though my travels have taken me far
and have aged me.

Have you remained the same spark of light
as when God placed you in me?
Or have you grown with me
across these countless years of living?

Many adventures have we been on,
many moments touched hand over hand,
turning to one another with deep smiles
that know the blessing of an eternal love.

TRUE WIND

When the wind calls to me again,
like a messenger of God,
I will follow it.
I need no storm or rushing gale
to move me.
Only a soft and gentle touch
that does not ask me to move, or change.

No, this wind is the True Wind,
for it loves me as I am.

A BIRD

Once I was a bird,
and will be so after.
First in ignorance,
and later in Truth.

FOOTSTEPS

My heart has become soft and warm with you.
Old habits have fallen away,
without clinging.

The passageway of truth in me is well worn,
so that my footsteps are more certain,
and I fear less getting lost in the dark.

HERE TO STAY

The heart given to me,
offered for my renewal,
is here to stay.
No need to turn away or close.

HOLINESS

When I come to this place, I cry.
My Child, the Child in me,
who is my joy and my blessing, cries.
That is how I know this is a home—
a sacred, holy place.
I feel no need to guard myself or hold back my truth.
I let my layers shed here.
And it is not even I who gives permission;
the permission is already given,
and I open myself to receive.

Upon returning,
I feel how much my Child loves this.
It is he, my soul, that cries in joy,
"We have found the place where we are free."
I do not try to understand it;
I just simply come to where we may be free.
And in feeling and grieving,
and opening,
we return to the presence of God.
And God opens up to me like a flower,
and God opens *me* like a flower,
and we sing in the sweet rain of holiness.

IN SILENCE

The wind speaks to me in silence.
I cannot tell you what it says,
or what it wants;

only that it brings me to a place
where I can know myself.
And that is enough.

STARS

My Father said each star is a Child,
and each Child a star.
We are all Children of the Living God,
stars upon stars that shine forever.

THE GARDEN

The other day my Child led me into the Garden.
I trusted him, and where he was taking me,
for his memory of You is far greater than my own.

IN GLORY

The mist that came in the morning,
that blanketed the ground outside my window,
was singing a sweet, alluring melody.
"Rise my love, whom I do love.
Today is the day when all the earth shall rise in glory."
Sunlight touched the mist with endearment,
and it lit up in a heavenly glow.

I put on my slippers and walked outside,
and the whole world sang in chorus.
Sure enough, I sang too,
words I had not known, but which came up from in me.
It was when I sang with all the earth
that I was no longer a witness, but a part of it.

I was the mist that held me in love.
I was the sunlight that shone upon me with endearment.
I was the grass and flowers that sprang up to be kissed.
I was the whole earth rising in glory.

HEART OF LOVE

Good Lord, I'm free.

Have you heard today?
That the world has broken down in the Heart of Love?
That we have once again become children
playing in the ever-golden light?

INFINITE

Who I am in this moment
is not who I was in the last.
The stories have fallen away,
and I have been lifted above
the river of my thoughts.

Time is of no measure.
Form moves around me,
but I am not of form.
Wind and light touch my body,
but I am not the wind, nor the light,
nor my body.

I have merged with the Infinite,
if only for this moment,
this instant,
this hour.

ALREADY THERE

In the light
we need not create,
for we *are already there*.

AWAKE

To be awake;
what a blessing it is to be awake.

I see the light of morning, warming the earth.
I feel the delicate texture of paper, carpet, skin.
I hear my lover's voice and listen to her when she speaks.

Oh, what a blessing it is to be awake.

NO END IN YOU

My soul knows no end in You,
for in You there is no end in him.
I become a field stretched out beneath the sun,
and my Child dances playfully.

AS I AM

Here,
like the old who have come before me,
like a never-ending sun
in a universe I have never known,
I am free to be as I am
and cast off my clothes.

AT THE END

At the end,
when You have opened my eyes
and lifted me from my heavy seat,
I'll know it was from the same love
You gave to me in the beginning.

A Child I was born,
and a Child I will return.

www.ingramcontent.com/pod-product-compliance
Lightning Source LLC
Chambersburg PA
CBHW060620080526
44585CB00013B/912